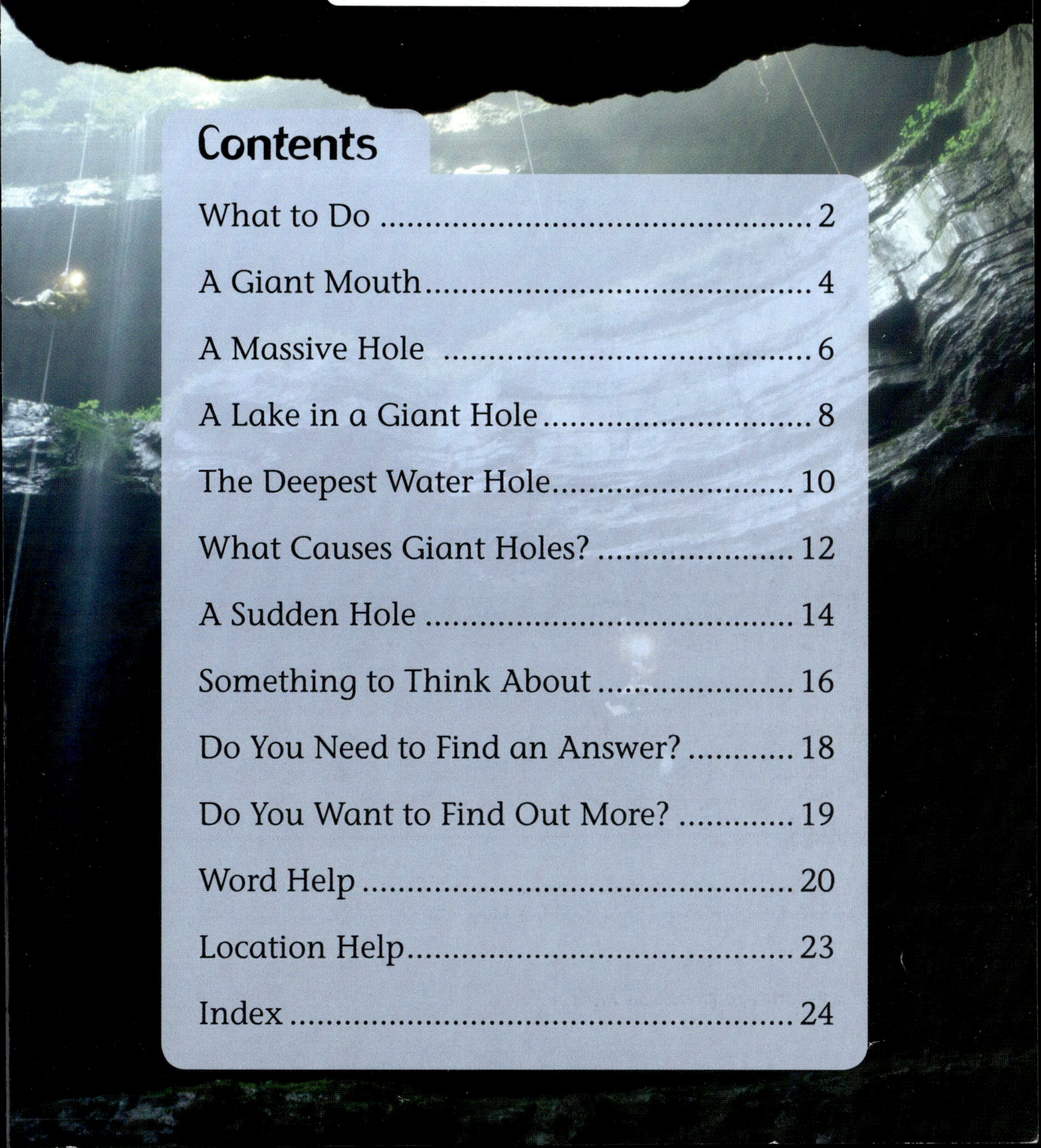

Contents

What to Do

Choose a face

Remember the colour you have chosen.

When you see your face on the page, you are the LEADER.

The LEADER reads the text in the speech bubbles.

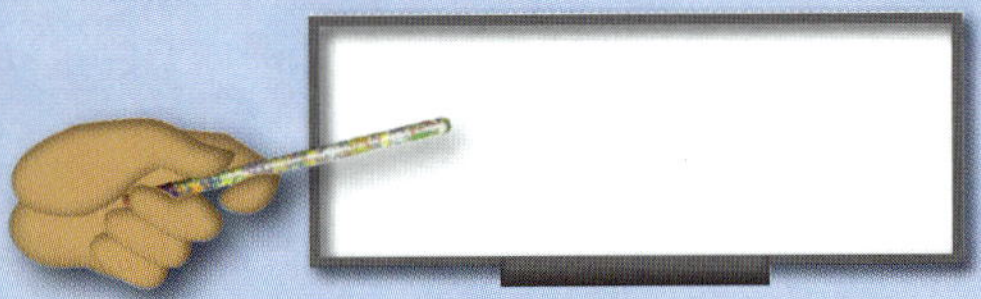

There are extra words and questions to help you on the teacher's whiteboard. The LEADER reads these aloud.

When you see this stop sign, the LEADER reads it aloud.

You might need:

- to look at the WORD HELP on pages 20–22;
- to look at the LOCATION HELP on page 23;
- an atlas.

If you are the **LEADER**, follow these steps:

1 PREDICT

Think about what is on the page.

- Say to your group:

"I am looking at this page and I think it is going to be about…"

- Tell your group:

"Read the page to yourselves."

2 CLARIFY

Talk about words and their meaning.

- Say to your group:

"Are there any words you don't know?"

"Is there anything else on the page you didn't understand?"

- Talk about the words and their meanings with your group.
- Read the whiteboard.

- Ask your group to find the LET'S CHECK word in the WORD HELP on pages 20–22. Ask them to read the meaning of the word aloud.

3 ASK QUESTIONS

Talk about how to find out more.

- Say to your group:

"Who has a question about what we have read?"

- Question starters are: how…, why…, when…, where…, what…, who…
- Read the question on the whiteboard and talk about it with your group.

4 SUMMARISE

Think about who and what the story was mainly about.

When you get to pages 16–17, you can talk to a partner or write and draw on your own.

 or 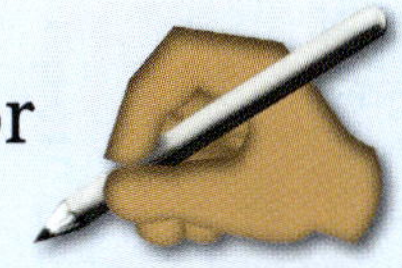

A Giant Mouth

I am looking at this page and I think it is going to be about… because...

Sinkholes happen when the ground falls in and leaves a big hole. They can be found all over the world. Some are small and not very deep. Others are very wide and very deep.

Sinkholes can take many years to **form**. Some, however, just happen suddenly. The ground can open up like a giant mouth and swallow everything near it.

Are there any words you don't know?

Let's check: form

Who has a question about what we have read?

Why do you think some sinkholes take many years to form?

The Great Blue Hole is the largest ocean sinkhole in the world.

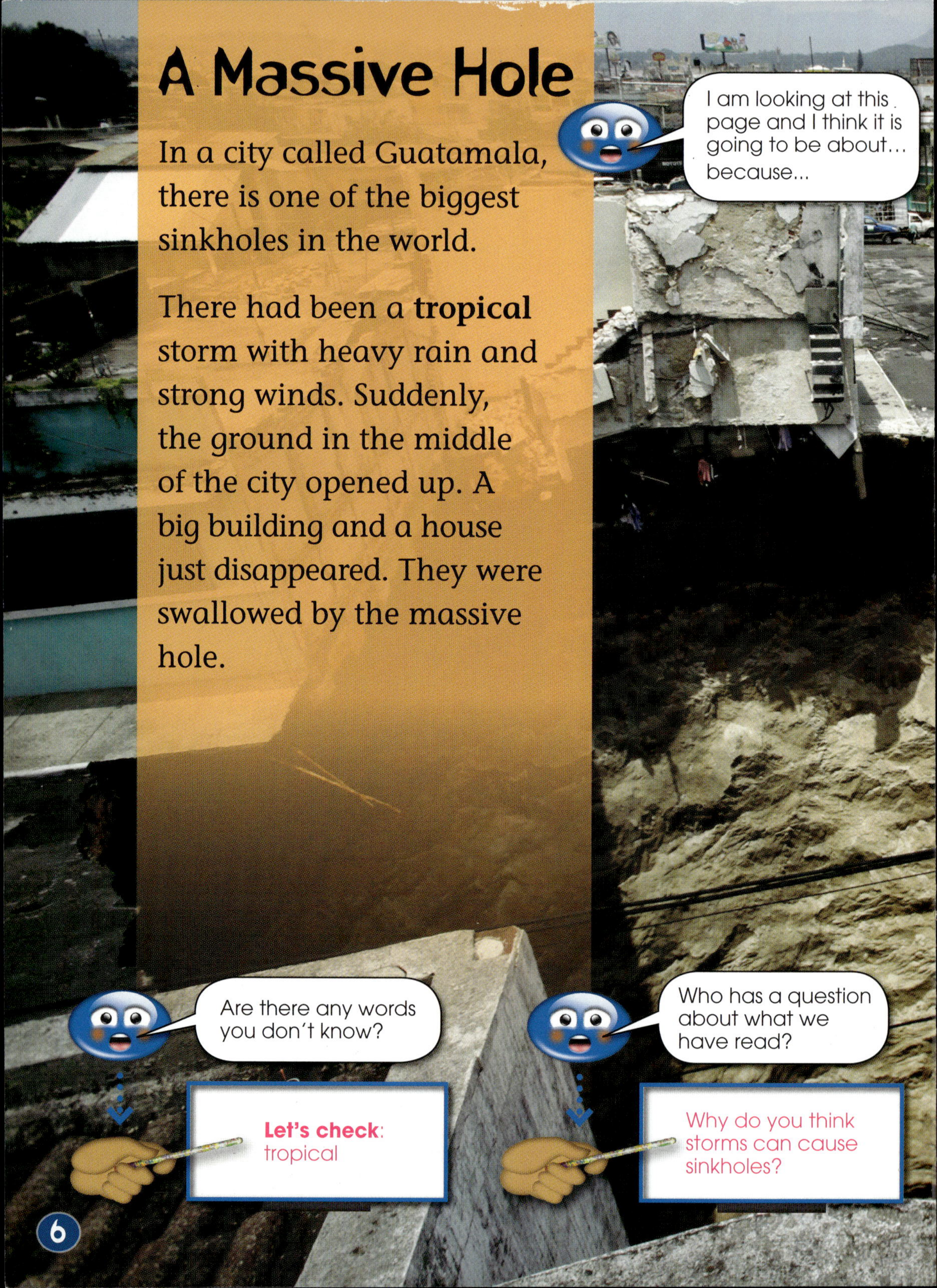

A Massive Hole

I am looking at this page and I think it is going to be about… because…

In a city called Guatamala, there is one of the biggest sinkholes in the world.

There had been a **tropical** storm with heavy rain and strong winds. Suddenly, the ground in the middle of the city opened up. A big building and a house just disappeared. They were swallowed by the massive hole.

Are there any words you don't know?

Let's check: tropical

Who has a question about what we have read?

Why do you think storms can cause sinkholes?

This huge sinkhole is about 18 metres wide and 100 metres deep.

A Lake in a Giant Hole

I am looking at this page and I think it is going to be about… because…

In a city called Winter Park, there is a beautiful lake. However, this lake was once an ugly hole.

One day, after a **drought**, the ground just **collapsed**. It left a very wide and deep hole.

The hole kept getting bigger and bigger. A swimming pool disappeared into it. Big buildings, trees and cars went tumbling into the hole, too.

Are there any words you don't know?

Let's check: collapsed

Who has a question about what we have read?

How do you think the sinkhole became a beautiful lake?

This sinkhole is now known as Lake Rose in Winter Park, Florida.

The Deepest Water Hole

I am looking at this page and I think it is going to be about… because…

In Mexico, there is a very deep hole that is filled with water. It is the deepest water hole in the world.

Scientists want to find out what is deep down in this hole. The hole is so deep, however, that divers have not been able to reach the bottom.

So the scientists **invented** a robot that can **explore** deep holes like this. It is able to go where no person can.

Are there any words you don't know?

Let's check: explore

Who has a question about what we have read?

Why do you think scientists want to explore the bottom of the hole?

Some people think that this deep hole could have been made when a volcano collapsed.

STOP
My predictions were right/wrong because . . .

This page was mainly about
fact
fact

What Causes Giant Holes?

I am looking at this page and I think it is going to be about… because…

Sinkholes can happen in different ways. In some places, there is a soft rock under the ground called **limestone**. Water can eat away at the rock. The ground will collapse if there is no rock underneath to hold it up.

Water pipes under the ground can break. All the water can make the ground collapse.

Some people even think that **meteorites** have made holes!

Are there any words you don't know?

Let's check: meteorites

Who has a question about what we have read?

How do you think a broken water pipe could cause a sinkhole?

This sinkhole appeared when an underground cave collapsed.

This page was mainly about
fact
fact

STOP
My predictions were right/wrong because . . .

A Sudden Hole

I am looking at this page and I think it is going to be about… because…

Sinkholes that happen without **warning** can be very dangerous. Sometimes, roads have collapsed and traffic has been **gobbled** up.

People have disappeared into sinkholes, too.

No one can be sure when the ground might open up like a giant mouth and swallow everything nearby. Sinkholes are **rare**, however. A person would be very unlucky to fall into one.

Are there any words you don't know?

Let's check: warning

Who has a question about what we have read?

Why might it be difficult to escape from a sinkhole?

This parked bus was suddenly gobbled up by a sinkhole.

This page was mainly about
fact
fact

STOP
My predictions were right/wrong because . . .

Something to Think About

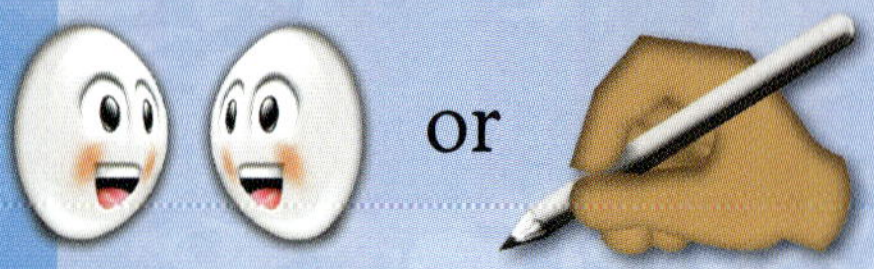

Think about what you have read about sinkholes. Can you remember what happens, and what the causes are? Talk about your ideas with a partner, or write them down.

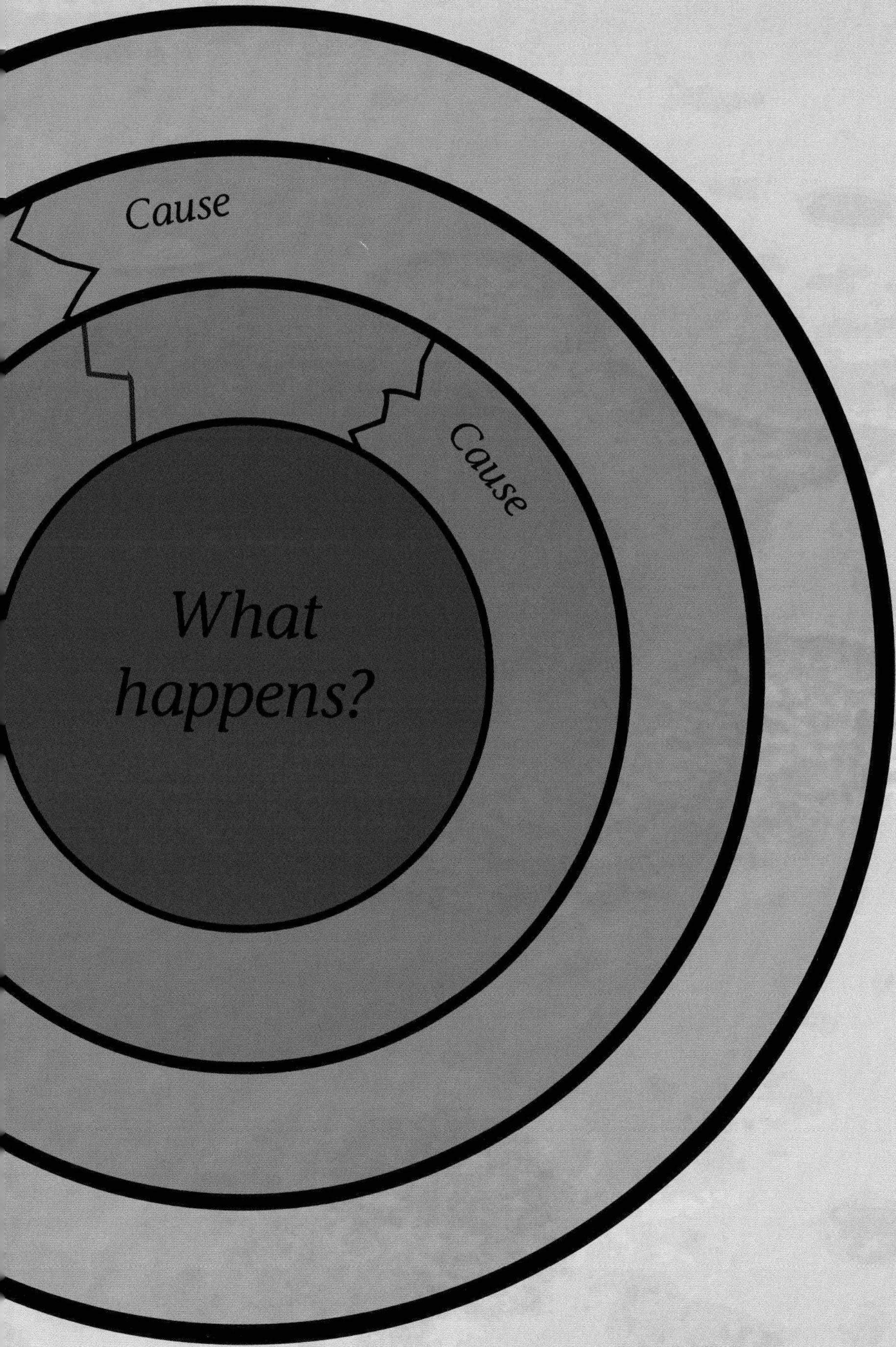
Cause
Cause
What happens?

Do You Need to Find an Answer?

You could go to . . .

Do You Want to Find Out More?

You could look in books or on the internet. These key words could help you:

DEPTHX robot

Great Blue Hole

Guatemala sinkhole

Lake Rose, Florida

sinkholes

Word Help

Dictionary

collapsed	fell down suddenly
drought	a long time without rain
explore	to look carefully around a place and learn about it
form	to take shape
gobbled	ate something quickly
invented	made something that no one else had made
limestone	a rock formed mostly from shells and other animal remains
meteorites	pieces of rock that have reached the Earth from outer space

sinkholes	huge holes in the ground, made when the earth collapses in one spot
tropical	the hot and humid weather patterns found in the warmest parts of the world
warning	telling someone to be careful

Word Help

Thesaurus

disappeared	vanished
explore	investigate, look into
massive	huge, enormous, gigantic
suddenly	unexpectedly, hastily
tumbling	falling, plunging

Location Help

Where Are These Giant Holes?

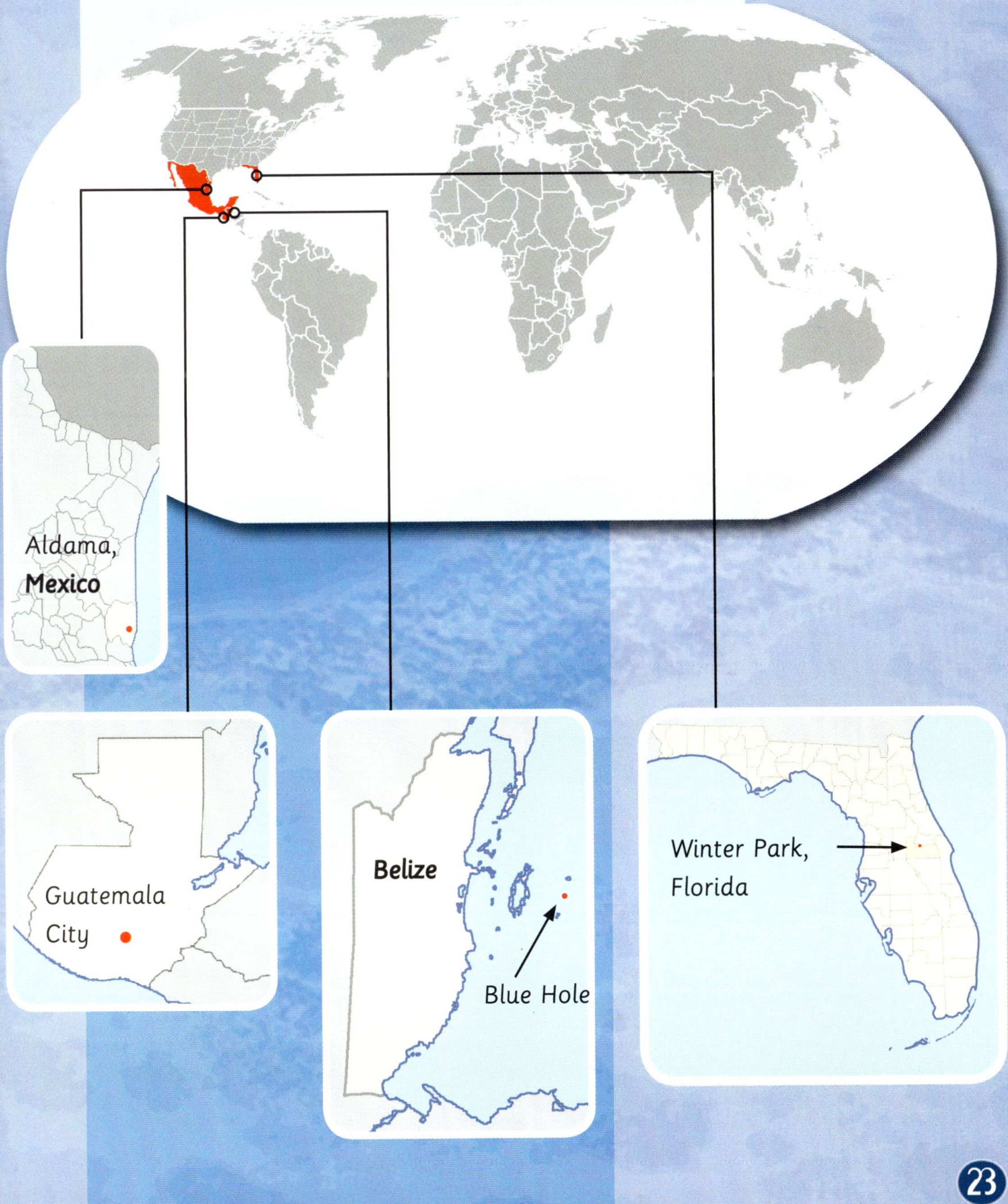

Index